CONTENTS

	Page	(Vocal/Backing)
EXTRA RESOURCES/PERCUSSION	2	-
CAST LIST	3	-
SCRIPT and SONG LYRICS	4	-
FULL NARRATION (with songs)	-	1
SONGS (incl. percussion)		
Oh, Chicken Licken!	10	2 6
The Sky Is Falling	12	3 7
Foxy Loxy	16	4 8
Just A Little Acorn	19	5 9
COPYRIGHT INFORMATION	22	-

© 2012 Out of the Ark Ltd

Extra Resources

We have provided a number of extra resources to accompany this *'Song and Story'* book/CD. **To download the following, visit our website at www.outoftheark.co.uk/resources**.

- Story/script in a child-friendly font so children can read as they listen to the narrated story *(CD track 1)*
- Mini-books with simplified story (for easy reading) and space to illustrate the story
- Lyric sheets

Percussion Notes

Percussion parts are included for all the songs *(see music score)* and we have also suggested areas in the script where percussion can be used for sound effects. Encouraging the children to play along with the songs will enrich their musical experience, helping with co-ordination and teamwork. Have fun including as much as you like and experiment with making other 'instruments' from everyday objects you might find at home or in the classroom.

Cast List

Speaking parts:

Narrator — Suitable for an adult/older child, or easily divided into shorter sections for a number of different children.

Chicken L — Lots of pecking about and flapping of wings is needed for this role. Has a few short lines.

Friends — 7 children with confidence to play Henny Lenny, Cocky Locky, Ducky Lucky, Drakey Lakey, Goosey Loosey, Gander Lander and Turkey Lurkey. Each has a few short lines to deliver.

Foxy Loxy — Someone with a charming manner and a cheeky grin would be perfect! He needs to be smartly dressed with a bowler hat. Has a few short lines.

Ideas for non-speaking parts:

There are relatively few speaking parts in this musical, however there are lots of opportunities to involve more children throughout the play. The main body of your performers can stand in the 'choir', and as there is so much scope for using a variety of percussion *(see Percussion Notes)* you could create a percussion band and allocate each child an instrument. The choir and percussion band should also join in the unison lines of script. You could allocate others to set the scene:

The wood — This could be children at the back of the stage dressed in brown waving some homemade branches as Chicken Licken pecks about on the stage. The children would need to exit the stage as Chicken Licken runs out of the wood.

The fox's den — Use the children, dressed in appropriate colours or outfits, to make the den by forming a semi-circle at the side of the stage. Once the animals have all gone into the den, the children can close up the circle around them. As the animals are eaten, they can exit the stage through the back of the den and the fox can emerge from an empty den.

Script and Song Lyrics

NARRATOR   Once upon a time a little chicken called Chicken Licken went out for a walk. She walked all the way to the wood. It was a lovely autumn day and as she scratched and pecked about, an acorn fell down from a tree, straight on to her head.[1] Chicken Licken was very shocked. She flapped her wings, gave a big loud 'cluck' and shouted out.

CHICKEN L   The sky is falling, the sky is falling!

Song 1.   OH, CHICKEN LICKEN!   CD track 2/6

1   An acorn fell from the sky,
    It fell right down from on high.
    She got in a terrible flap!
    Oh, Chicken Licken,
    What was that?

2   An acorn fell small and brown,
    It made her jump off the ground.
    What on earth could it be?
    Oh, Chicken Licken,
    Deary me!

3   *Repeat verse 1*

© 2012 Out of the Ark Ltd, Middlesex TW12 2HD
CCLI Song No. 6010223

NARRATOR   Chicken Licken decided that she must go and tell the king immediately. So she rushed out of the wood and went off down the road.[2] Soon she met Henny Lenny.

HENNY L   Good morning Chicken Licken, where are you going?

CHICKEN L   The sky is falling. I am going to tell the king!

---

1 **Added percussion:** Use a woodblock for the falling acorn and lots of shakers and guiros when Chicken Licken flaps her wings.
2 **Added percussion:** Lightly shake a box of small pebbles each time the characters walk down the road.

HENNY L	Can I come too?
CHICKEN L	Of course you can.
NARRATOR	So Chicken Licken and Henny Lenny went on down the road.[2] Soon they met Cocky Locky.
COCKY L	Good morning Chicken Licken, where are you going?
ALL	The sky is falling. We are going to tell the king!
COCKY L	Can I come too?
FRIENDS	Of course you can. *(This line, each time it occurs, is spoken by Chicken Licken and the friends she's already collected on her way)*
NARRATOR	So Chicken Licken, Henny Lenny and Cocky Locky went on down the road.[2] Soon they met Ducky Lucky.
DUCKY L	Good morning Chicken Licken, where are you going?
ALL	The sky is falling. We're going to tell the king!
DUCKY L	Can I come too?
FRIENDS	Of course you can.
NARRATOR	So Chicken Licken, Henny Lenny, Cocky Locky and Ducky Lucky went on down the road.[2] Soon they met Drakey Lakey.
DRAKEY L	Good morning Chicken Licken, where are you going?
ALL	The sky is falling. We're going to tell the king!
DRAKEY L	Can I come too?
FRIENDS	Of course you can.
NARRATOR	So Chicken Licken, Henny Lenny, Cocky Locky, Ducky Lucky and Drakey Lakey went on down the road.[2]

Song 2.   THE SKY IS FALLING   CD track 3/7

1 We're off to tell the king,
   We're off to tell the king.
   Will you come along with us?
   We're off to tell the king.

   CHORUS   *'Cos the sky is falling,*
                 The sky is falling,
                 The sky is falling,
                 Down, down, down.

2 Oh, don't go to the wood,
   Oh, don't go to the wood.
   Turn around and come with us
   And don't go to the wood.

   CHORUS

3 *Repeat verse 1*

   CHORUS   *'Cos the sky is falling,*
                 The sky is falling,
                 The sky is falling,
                 Down, down, down.
                 The sky is falling,
                 The sky is falling,
                 The sky is falling,
                 Down, down, down.

   © 2012 Out of the Ark Ltd, Middlesex TW12 2HD
   CCLI Song No. 6010230

NARRATOR   Soon they met Goosey Loosey.

GOOSEY L   Good morning Chicken Licken, where are you going?

ALL   The sky is falling. We're going to tell the king!

GOOSEY L   Can I come too?

FRIENDS   Of course you can.

NARRATOR   So Chicken Licken, Henny Lenny, Cocky Locky, Ducky Lucky,
                Drakey Lakey and Goosey Loosey went on down the road.[2]
                Soon they met Gander Lander.

GANDER L	Good morning Chicken Licken, where are you going?
ALL	The sky is falling. We're going to tell the king!
GANDER L	Can I come too?
FRIENDS	Of course you can.
NARRATOR	So Chicken Licken, Henny Lenny, Cocky Locky, Ducky Lucky, Drakey Lakey, Goosey Loosey and Gander Lander went on down the road.[2] Soon they met Turkey Lurkey.
TURKEY L	Good morning Chicken Licken, where are you going?
ALL	The sky is falling. We're going to tell the king!
TURKEY L	Can I come too?
FRIENDS	Of course you can.
NARRATOR	So Chicken Licken, Henny Lenny, Cocky Locky, Ducky Lucky, Drakey Lakey, Goosey Loosey, Gander Lander and Turkey Lurkey all went on down the road.[2] As they walked, a fine gentleman came into view. He was smartly dressed with a bowler hat and was very well spoken. His name was Foxy Loxy.
FOXY L	Good morning Chicken Licken, where are you going?
ALL	The sky is falling. We're going to tell the king!
FOXY L	Do you know the way?
ALL	No.
FOXY L	Come with me. I will show you the way.

Song 3.   FOXY LOXY   CD track 4/8

1 Somebody's walking down the road,
   Looking smart from head to toe.
   Somebody's walking down the road,
   I think it's Foxy Loxy.

2 Oh, he looks such a charming chap,
  With a crisp white collar and a bowler hat.
  Oh, he looks such a charming chap,
  I think it's Foxy Loxy.

3 Friendly and courteous without fail,
  With his whiskers fine and his bushy tail.
  Friendly and courteous without fail,
  I think it's Foxy Loxy.

4 *Repeat verse 1*

© 2012 Out of the Ark Ltd, Middlesex TW12 2HD
CCLI Song No. 6010261

NARRATOR   So Chicken Licken, Henny Lenny, Cocky Locky, Ducky Lucky, Drakey Lakey, Goosey Loosey, Gander Lander and Turkey Lurkey all went on down the road with Foxy Loxy.[2] Then Foxy Loxy led them through some fields.

ALL   Through some fields.[3]

NARRATOR   Over a big hill.

ALL   Over a big hill. [4]

NARRATOR   Through a forest.

ALL   Through a forest.[5]

NARRATOR   *(Full of suspense)* And all the way to his den.

ALL   *(Full of suspense)* And all the way to his den.[6]

FOXY L   Here we are!

---

3 **Added percussion:** Use a sandblock to create the sound of the characters walking through the fields.
4 **Added percussion:** Use a swanee whistle (or alternatively panpipes or a kazoo) to create the sound effect of going over the hill.
5 **Added percussion:** Scrunch up some noisy paper in your hands to represent them walking through the forest.
6 **Added percussion:** Rub cymbals together while this line is spoken, gradually getting louder and finishing with a huge crash.

NARRATOR   So Chicken Licken, Henny Lenny, Cocky Locky, Ducky Lucky, Drakey Lakey, Goosey Loosey, Gander Lander and Turkey Lurkey walked into Foxy Loxy's den, and naughty Foxy Loxy gobbled them all up for dinner![7] *(See staging ideas on page 3)*

FOXY L   *(Comes out of his den and rubs his tummy)* Very tasty!

NARRATOR   So Chicken Licken, Henny Lenny, Cocky Locky, Ducky Lucky, Drakey Lakey, Goosey Loosey, Gander Lander and Turkey Lurkey never got to tell the king that the sky was falling.

Song 4.   JUST A LITTLE ACORN   CD track 5/9

1   Just a little acorn
    To scare them all to bits,
    But as for Foxy Loxy,
    He just sat in his chair
    And licked his lips!

2   They thought the sky was falling,
    You should have seen them run,
    But as for Foxy Loxy,
    He just sat in his chair
    And said, 'Yum, yum!'

3   They were a little silly
    Getting so confused,
    But as for Foxy Loxy,
    He just sat in his chair
    And had a snooze.

4   *Repeat verse 1*

    © 2012 Out of the Ark Ltd, Middlesex TW12 2HD
    CCLI Song No. 6010278

---

7 **Added percussion:** Scrape a stick across a guiro for the fox's eating noise.

Oh, Chicken Licken!

Words and Music by
Niki Davies

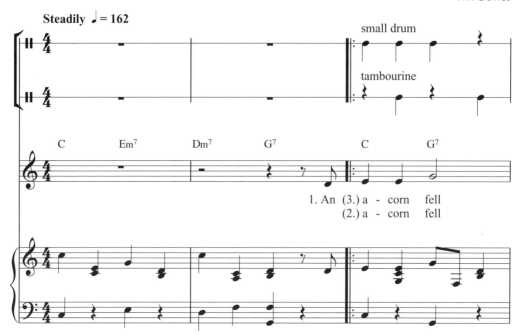

© 2012 Out of the Ark Ltd, Middlesex TW12 2HD
CCLI Song No. 6010223

The Sky Is Falling

Words and Music by
Niki Davies

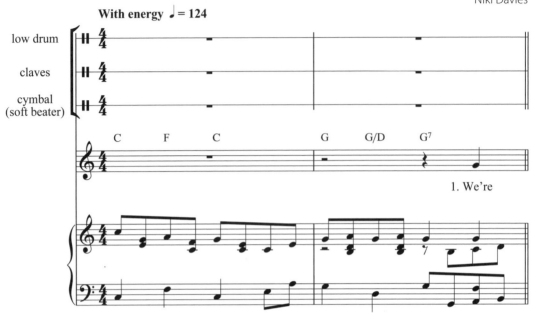

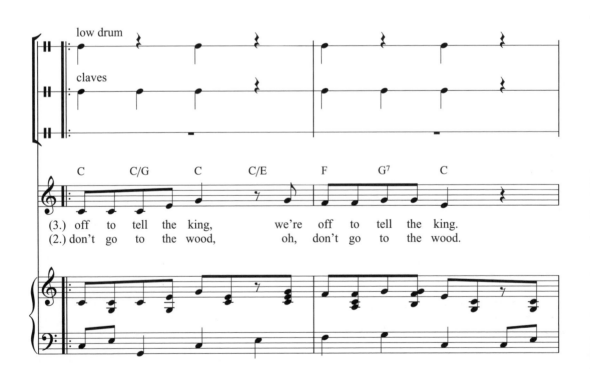

© 2012 Out of the Ark Ltd, Middlesex TW12 2HD
CCLI Song No. 6010230

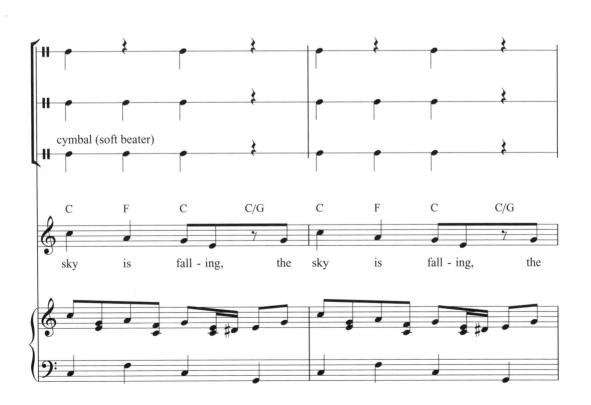

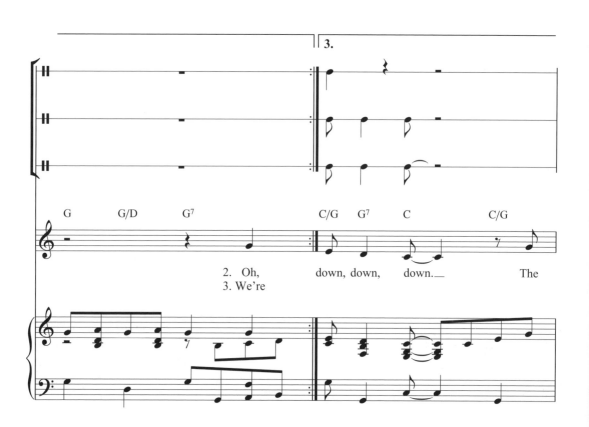

Foxy Loxy

Words and Music by
Niki Davies

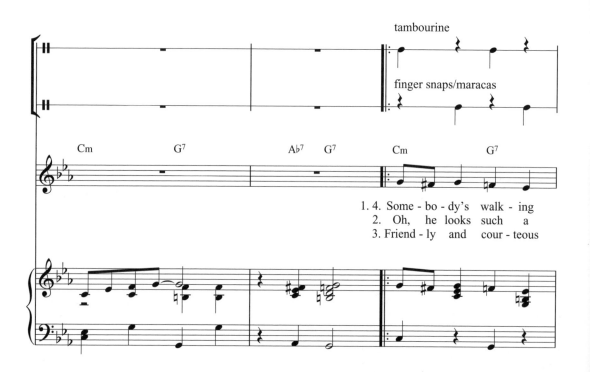

© 2012 Out of the Ark Ltd, Middlesex TW12 2HD
CCLI Song No. 6010261

Just A Little Acorn

Words and Music by
Niki Davies

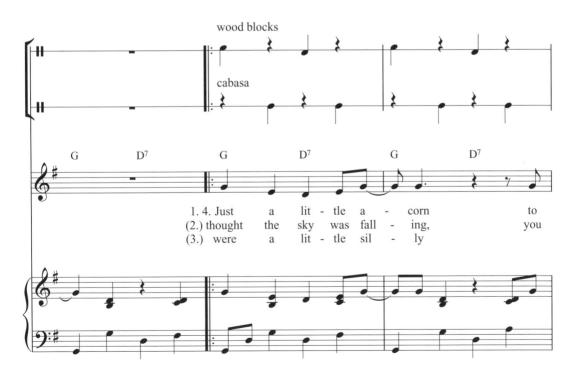

1. 4. Just a lit-tle a-corn to
(2.) thought the sky was fall-ing, you
(3.) were a lit-tle sil-ly

© 2012 Out of the Ark Ltd, Middlesex TW12 2HD
CCLI Song No. 6010278

Copyright & Licensing

VERY IMPORTANT

You are free to use the material in our musicals for all teaching purposes. However, the performance of musicals or songs to an audience and the reproduction of scripts, lyrics and music scores are subject to licensing requirements by law. A free licence for certain performances is provided with this songbook/CD package – see below for details.

Helpful information about licensing can also be found on the following website:

'A Guide to Licensing Copyright in Schools' www.licensing-copyright.org

And remember, we're happy to help. For advice contact our customer services team:

UK: 020 8481 7200   International: +44 20 8481 7200   copyright@outoftheark.com

---

(1) Performance of Musicals

The performance of a work involving drama, movement, narrative or dialogue such as a musical requires a specific licence from the publisher. **Your PRS licence does not cover musicals.**

If your school is performing *'Chicken Licken'* by Niki Davies as a musical on school premises, to an audience of staff, pupils and/or their families, then to simplify the process we have already issued an inclusive licence that grants permission to stage a performance.

If you are performing *'Chicken Licken'* for any other type of audience please contact Out of the Ark Music directly to apply for a performance licence.

(2) Licensing of Audio and Video Recordings

Copying Out of the Ark Music's audio CDs is not permitted without obtaining a licence from the publisher. File-sharing or installation of Out of the Ark Music's audio CD tracks on to a computer are strictly forbidden. To make an audio or video recording please contact Out of the Ark Music directly.

(3) Other use of the published material

If you are not staging a musical but still intend to use material from the publication then different licences are required:

(a) Reproduction of Song Lyrics or Musical Scores
The following licences from Christian Copyright Licensing Ltd (www.ccli.com) permit photocopying or reproduction of song lyrics and music scores, for example to create song-sheets, overhead transparencies or to use any electronic display medium.

For UK schools: 'Collective Worship Copyright Licence' and 'Music Reproduction Licence.'
For churches: 'Church Copyright and Music Reproduction Licence.'

Please ensure that you log the songs that are used on your copy report. (Organisations that do not hold one of the above licences should contact Out of the Ark Music directly for permission.)

(b) Performance of Songs
If you are not staging a musical but are performing any of our songs for the public on school premises (ie for anybody other than staff and pupils) then royalty payments become due. Most schools have an arrangement with the Performing Rights Society (PRS) through their local authority. Organisations that do not have such an arrangement should contact Out of the Ark Music directly.

by Niki Davies

Far more than just a songbook, this wonderful series of traditional stories has been written for use in nurseries, reception and at home. The well-loved tales are re-told through a very simple script and just a few bite-size songs.

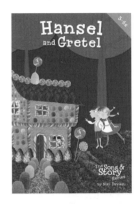

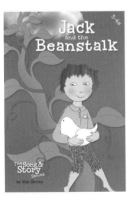

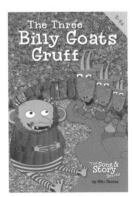

Listen, read, sing, perform!

Out of the Ark Music
Kingsway Business Park, Oldfield Road, Hampton, Middlesex TW12 2HD, UK
Tel: +44 (0)20 8481 7200 **Fax:** +44 (0)20 8941 5548
Email: info@outoftheark.com www.outoftheark.com

Out of the Ark Music
listen online at www.outoftheark.com

The My World Series

Catchy songs that are fun to sing!

The 'My World' series is written by a team of top children's writers, which includes Niki Davies, Alison Hedger, Paul Field and Mark and Helen Johnson. Developed specifically for pre-school and infant children, each book includes **12 catchy songs**, plus **extra teaching material** and an **accompanying audio CD**.

I Love Maths

This action-packed collection of songs will help make learning about numbers and shapes great fun. Jump on the Number Bus; count sleeps until your birthday; and learn about fractions as you eat a pizza. With songs covering number combinations, doubling, rounding up and down, your 5x table and much more.

Toys & Games

A sparkling collection of catchy songs to help children learn about their favourite toys and games. Let their imagination run wild as they do the *Teddy-Bear Rock*, imagine life with a robot and become a Jack-in-a-box. Covering topics such as old toys, new toys, skipping and dressing up, there's even a song to sing as you tidy it all away!

Space

An out-of-this-world collection of songs about Space. Targeted towards a slightly older age group, it is suitable for children up to nine years of age, helping them learn as they sing about our universe, the planets, the sun and moon, rockets, gravity and the odd alien!

People Who Help Us

A fantastic collection of songs about all kinds of people who help us day by day, from the postman to the lollipop lady and the plumber to the teacher!

Colours & Patterns

A collection of vibrant new songs with themes including colours of the rainbow, animal patterns, colour-mixing, design and doodling and all things black and white. So grab your paintbrush, get singing and 'open your eyes to the colours of the world'.

Wonderful Water

This fabulous collection of new songs will have you thinking, singing and learning from beginning to end. We splash in it, wash in it, play in it, grow with it! What would we do without Wonderful Water?

Minibeasts

Your imagination can run wild with this collection of original songs taking you into the exciting world of slimy slugs, buzzy bees, spinning spiders, pitter patter caterpillars, not to mention snails and blue-bottles!

Taking Care of Myself

A wonderful collection of simple, well-crafted songs with fantastic accompaniments. Children will love to sing about bath time, road safety, eating sweets and even going to the dentist!

On The Move

A collection of exciting songs all about transport, going places and how things move. What happens when you drive a car with square wheels? How many ways are there to get to school? However you travel, these songs are guaranteed to get you moving!

Animals

A collection of superb songs that will help you learn as you sing with all its amazing facts about animals. With a wide variety of themes, including dinosaurs, baby animals, pets, habitats and animal sounds, there's something for everyone. We've even thrown in a dragon for good measure!

Out of the Ark Music
Kingsway Business Park, Oldfield Road, Hampton, Middlesex TW12 2HD, UK
Tel: +44(0)20 8481 7200 **Fax:** +44(0)20 8941 5548 **Email:** info@outoftheark.com
www.outoftheark.com